Moving On

TEMPTATION

Bob & Jill Moffett
TEMPTATION

Scripture Union
130 City Road, London EC1V 2NJ

© 1984 Bob and Jill Moffett

First published 1984

ISBN 0 86201 225 2

Phototypeset by J & L Composition Limited, Filey
Printed in Great Britain at The Pitman Press, Bath

Contents

Are you being got at?
Have you ever tried to break a bad habit?
Have you ever thought God is asking too much of you?
Have you wondered what is really 'right' or 'wrong'?
How would you feel if others could see your thoughts?
Do you sometimes feel that your Christian life is in reverse gear?
Do you feel like Saint Paul when he said:

> *'I don't do the good I want to;*
> *instead I do the evil that I do*
> *not want to do.' (Romans 7:19)*

IF SO, THIS BOOK IS FOR YOU ... READ ON

Preface

John Grayston, editor at Scripture Union, wrote to us asking if we would consider writing a book on the 'Second Coming of Jesus' or 'Temptation'. After due consideration and prayer, we replied along these lines: 'Seeing as the former has not happened and that we know more about the latter (temptation) we would agree to have a try! We have not found this book easy because of the temptation of 'indiscipline' – we have been learning (tempted) as we have gone along.

It is not meant in any way to be a complete 'answer' to the problems of temptation but to give some general guidelines.

Our thanks to Professor Duncan Vere for his assistance on 'Body Movement'; to Rev. Martin Wallace for 'Letters From Down Under'; George Brucks for the thinking on the 'Yes Factor' and to Dominic Swords for compiling a Survey Questionnaire, the results of which have been a factor in our writing.

Finally our gratitude to Jacqui Church and June Moult for typing the manuscripts from our scrawl.

To all those we have led into temptation over the writing of this book we apologise, and hope that the reading of it will go a small way to putting the wrongs right!

Bob and Jill Moffett
Easter 1984

1

What is temptation?

From childhood days many of us have 'churned' out in our school assemblies often without any realisation, the words from the Lord's prayer, 'And lead us not into temptation'.

These days with all the stress of fat-free diets perhaps the word is used more than ever. 'Just look at that trifle – it looks so tempting.' We are continually bombarded by advertisements trying to persuade us to be tempted into eating, doing or buying something. Their business is certainly not easy, for what tempts one of us may be quickly disregarded by someone else. We have to be attracted to something in order to be tempted.

Do you, for example, ever feel tempted to stay in bed to the last second before you tell yourself you must get up? 'I can pray and read my Bible tonight, just a few more minutes' sleep will make me feel so much better through the day – besides it's cold out of bed.' To some people this would be no temptation at all, for they may hate staying in bed and would far rather be on a two-mile jog and have some prayer and Bible reading all before your alarm goes off. But then, on the other hand, perhaps they detest sleep.

Without restriction or pressure from society temptation is limited. If it was the 'norm' for your society to eat chocolate every moment of the day, the temptation to eat chocolate would not be a real one to you; it is more likely that you would be sick of the stuff! But in a society where all the

consequences of eating excessive chocolate – becoming fat, getting spots, suffering migraines – are constantly emphasised, a great yearning for chocolate and the ability to acquire it enable eating it to become a real temptation.

As Christians we are 'born again' and want to live as God wants us to. God doesn't want to put a new cover over us, to dress us up. He wants to start from within, by renewing our minds and giving us new values.

We therefore have a whole new set of guidelines. No longer are we living to please ourselves, we want to please God. We might now find that our temptations change as we become more concerned with what God wants and less with what we want. The desire to blaspheme is no concern to the non-Christian but to Christians with a growing awareness of God and a desire to respect him it may become a temptation with real and destructive force.

Is temptation sin?

Temptation itself is not wrong; it is the giving in to it which is wrong and which saddens the Lord.

I was visiting a local clergyman to talk about our recently commenced youth organisation in his area. As I was sipping my coffee the clergyman leant over towards me and said, 'Are you ever tempted to doubt God?' My immediate reaction was to give him an impressive answer as this meeting was crucial for the youth work. I knew, however, that in some quieter moments I had been tempted to doubt. After what seemed an endless pause I said, 'Yes, sometimes I am tempted to doubt God'. The clergyman's reaction was clear and I will never forget how he took my hand saying, 'That's a relief, so am I'.

The relief in the realisation that others are tempted just as we are is incredible. Many feel guilty because they are tempted. But all they are doing when they freely admit they are tempted is to recognise that they are normal human beings.

Our main worry should not be temptation but the sin into which the temptation can lead us. They are not the same. Sin is the surrendering to the temptation – in an action, a thought, or even a silence.

Simon and Jane were faced with the temptation not to say anything as the pizza they were buying went unnoticed amongst the other groceries at the checkout. Both of them knew the cashier had failed to ring the pizza price on the bill, and their telling glances showed that each knew that the other also knew. 'Of course the deceit was not intentional and it was not our mistake. Anyway, it's a bit embarrassing these days to be honest and it will be a small saving on the groceries this week.'

Now the temptation in itself was not wrong but within the next few seconds while waiting for the completed bill, Simon and Jane would make a choice to sin or not to sin. Their choice of silence was their consenting to the temptation and the result was sin.

The action not only wronged the supermarket but also saddened God. Any sin that we commit spoils our relationship with God. We may get away with it at the supermarket but we cannot get away with it in the eyes of God. Take a look at Psalm 139 where God's knowledge and care for us are wonderfully shown.

Temptations are not something to be frowned upon. It is very easy to feel that as a Christian you are not getting anywhere – the temptations are too strong. Don't be saddened if you feel more and more temptations coming your way; rather be encouraged, and see them as things that are important to your growth as a Christian. Temptation can bring out the worst or the best in us. It does not leave us the same; we will have moved forwards or backwards. In fact, although it may be difficult to believe at times, our temptations will demonstrate and strengthen the love we have for God.

Temptation is therefore essential for the development of our Christian characters. God's purpose is to make us like Jesus, his Son.

Perhaps one of the best ways of seeing what temptation really is, is shown clearly in the first temptation. Read on to see how it all started.

2

No cover up
Adam and Eve

Adam and Eve started it off ... in more ways than one!
The Bible never does a cover up over the nasty bits. That's
one of the reasons that the Bible is so popular. It reveals the
good, the bad and the ugly of different individuals and races
in their search for God; it doesn't ignore the greed, lust and
unfaithfulness of God's people. It tells the story as it
happened.

Adam and Eve don't come off lightly – they get the full
coverage. God creates a world which is perfect. In this new
creation God makes man and breathes life into his nostrils
and the man begins to live (Genesis 2:7). In this paradise
where all appears to be going well, God informs Adam that
he can walk freely around picking fruit from any tree, except
one, 'the tree that gives knowledge of what is good and what
is bad' (2:16,17). Despite all this beauty, however, man
remains lonely and God makes Eve to be his companion and
they are to be mutually dependent on each other. Please read
Genesis 3:1–13.

The writer builds up the picture and then he drops the
bombshell – the disobedience of man. If it was not so serious,
it could sound like a Christmas pantomime. In the first 'Act'
the scene is set with all the characters enjoying peace and
happiness ... Then in Act One, Scene Two comes the arrival

of the wicked witch to a great noise of boos! from the audience. The wicked witch, in this case is the snake ('the most cunning animal that the Lord had made', 3:1) which arrives and begins the enticement ... 'when you eat it you will be like God and know what is good and what is bad' (3:5). Notice how this temptation was attractive ('the woman saw how beautiful the tree was and how good its fruit would be to eat') and also how mentally stimulating it was: '... you will be like God'.

We can learn a lot from this first temptation. *First*, visually it is very powerful ... 'the woman saw' (3:6). A lot of our temptations begin with what we see. This is not the sin. It's what we decide to do with what we see that determines whether it is going to lead us into sin or not.

Secondly, the inducement of the 'forbidden' is always appealing. 'Keep Off the Grass' signs are always a problem for Bob. 'Why should I?' he says. 'Who has the God-given right over grass?' The walled garden that has a notice saying 'KEEP OUT' is always an open invitation to view if there is a convenient peep-hole. The 'forbidden fruit', then, is always an attraction.

Thirdly, Eve listened to a creature rather than the Creator. Sometimes we prefer to listen to people rather than God because we prefer their advice ... they, after all are human and know what it's like to be tempted. Secretly we may also hope that they may condone what we really want to do. Of course we know that God's direction is better than anyone else's but ...

Eve followed her impressions. It sounded 'right'. She was accepting the deceit that the devil had placed before her. The argument seemed logical. It was attractive – why shouldn't she 'be like God'? It was impressive. She had not been presented with such a well reasoned argument before; but isn't that the cunning of the 'tempter' – he tries to make us believe that the action isn't quite so wrong anyway. When the man in the ticket office gives you 10p extra change with your train ticket you may very easily impress yourself with the reasoned argument that they make too much money anyway. Also that there was a time you bought a return ticket and never used the return half. And of course there was that unfortunate occasion when you lost your ticket and the ticket collector refused to believe you and you had to pay up. So the argument which you put forward impresses you to the point where the 10p gained is just the first contribution to the money lost in the past!

Fourthly, Eve made self-fulfilment her goal. The 'I' of what 'I' want is something that seems to be the bottom line for most of our temptations. Bob recently saw an advertisement for one of those super, fantastic, plug in, push button, memory, do-everything-for-you-without-lifting-the-receiver telephones. The argument went like this. 'If *we* had one of those Jilly, you would be able to push just one button to telephone most of your friends, you wouldn't have the hassle of looking up all those numbers. It looks more stylish and neater than the old one. We wouldn't have to pay rental on it to British Telecom etc. (It's only £59.95 – £40 off this month.)'

The truth was, Bob simply wanted a new 'toy' on his office desk; yes it would do all the things mentioned but he

15

did forget to mention how many years it would take before we were 'in' on the deal. There was nothing wrong with the 'old' one, and it was more than adequate, particularly as he was taking up a new position where he would use the phone less.

Finally, Eve 'took some of the fruit and ate it, then she gave some to Adam and he also ate it. As soon as they had eaten it, they were given understanding and realised that they were naked; so they sewed fig leaves together and covered themselves.' So simple the act, so hard the undoing. But the truth is that the mess created by a simple spur of the moment act, takes ages to disentangle. The first small lie of the moment necessitates further lies later on. The trusted employee who takes the loose change finds that his relationship with his employer is destroyed. The day off school to go out with your friends leads to the letter 'from your parents' in what appears very like your own handwriting. Giving in to the first temptation brings a whole host of others to bombard you.

There is also another danger – we often share our 'sin' (our direct rebellion against God) by involving others in it. It is bad enough to give in to temptation ourselves but it is far worse to lead someone else into it as well.

When God enters into this unhappy scene and asks Adam, 'Did you eat the fruit that I told you not to eat?' Adam's reply is familiar to us all: 'The woman you put here with me gave me the fruit, and I ate it.' Can you hear what is being said, loud and clear? 'It wasn't my fault, it was ... ' As soon as we give in to sin, and are confronted with it, there is always a very good reason why we are not responsible. The Lord God asked the woman, 'Why did you do this?' Eve then does exactly the same, 'The snake tricked me into eating it'.

When we give in to temptation we often try to pass the blame down or up the line.

Adam and Eve had been sold a false idea of good. They had been enticed with the belief that there was something beyond good and wisdom and sadly the bait had been taken and the lie that they would be like God became the saddest story of all time. The 'wicked witch' in our pantomime retreats, to the loud disgust of the watching world, into the background. But in real life the devil does not disappear altogether; on the contrary, he remains to make chaos in the lives of individuals and nations until his day of judgement.

Over the last few years there has been a strong emphasis on the suggestion that our 'actions' are very often a direct result of our environment – 'where we were brought up affects the way we behave'. It is, of course, true that our early surroundings do have a great impact on our later development but to some extent it is not the 'where' that is relevant but the 'how'. In any case it is wrong simply to 'blame' the system or our upbringing; God holds us individually responsible for our actions. Freedom has been given to us to make choices ... in the last analysis we cannot blame anyone else but ourselves.

Before the curtain comes down on this 'Act', God pronounces judgement (Genesis 3:14–21). This judgement is the direct result of Adam and Eve's action – they have rejected God's leadership and now have to struggle on their own. The 'buck-passing' has led to a complete mistrust of each other. Within their relationship 'to love and cherish' has become 'to desire and dominate' (see Genesis 3:16). The 'call of the jungle' mentality starts to take over. The world of paradise that captured our imagination in the first Act has given way to an estrangement from God and to a world of struggle, suffering and passionate human conflict.

3

No cover up
David and
Bathsheba

Perhaps one of the worst stories of lust, intrigue and murder
that we know is found in the Bible and involves one of the
most famous characters – King David. We have all heard the
story of David and Goliath. A young lad bringing a 'Red
Cross parcel' to his brothers on the front line, discovers that
the war is in a stalemate position. His brothers, like everybody else, sit around listening to the bellows of a giant called
Goliath challenging any nominated champion of the Israel-
ites to a fight to the death. The only problem is that no one
feels up to fighting this incredible hulk of a man, except, that
is, for David who offers his services to King Saul.

David's training to date has been a few scuffles with lions
and bears using a few stones and a sling – not quite the
strategic military establishment training required for this
task. King Saul in his desperation accepts David's offer and in
return offers him his own armour!

David, being a young shepherd boy, finds this all a bit too
much and decides that he will take his chances with an
unsophisticated catapult. Goliath's derision is clear. 'Come
on,' says Goliath, 'and I will give your body to birds and
animals to eat' (1 Samuel 17:44). But it was David with his
well-chosen and well-aimed stone who won the day, finally
removing Goliath's head with Goliath's own sword.

King Saul, in his delight at the subsequent victory over the fleeing Philistines, rewarded David with the hand of his daughter. But the delight turned to jealousy as the people acclaimed David with great honours.

So often success creates jealousy. Bob recalls someone at school who was good at every subject except for sport, at which he appeared to be a pathetic creature. Very few people liked him, however, not because of his personality, but simply because he was conscientious and clever. We were all jealous and secretly wished we had the 'brains' to do well. He happened to be Jewish and took a lot of 'stick' of a racial nature as well. All totally unfair of course but ...

Back to *our* success story: Saul falls from God's favour; God's prophet Samuel anoints David the shepherd boy who in turn becomes a very good friend of Jonathan, Saul's son. David is persecuted by Saul; Saul and his sons are killed by the Philistines and David is made King.

King David had made it to the top, had found favour with God and his people. But his downfall came in the Spring! Please read 2 Samuel 11.

'At the time of the year when kings usually go to war David sent out Joab with his officers and the Israelite army ...' (11:1).

The story starts with some irony; 'when kings usually go to war', David is at home! Yes, David is in the wrong place at the wrong time ... and that is when many of our temptations start. We place ourselves knowingly in a place where we are very vulnerable.

David gets up from his afternoon nap and takes a casual stroll on to the palace roof. As was the eastern custom the palace roof-top was always the highest point on the horizon, this being the king's privilege. And here the disastrous chain of events begins in earnest. King David looks out over the city and his eye is caught by a beautiful woman taking a bath.

What we see, as Eve and David both discovered, dictates much of our thought life, imaginations and dreams. David was tempted and revealed a common failure in many of us – lust, in his case for sexual gratification. Unfortunately the word lust has almost disappeared from our vocabulary; it seems a bit too sordid. We see two people who hardly know each other jumping into bed, and say 'they are making love'. It all sounds so nice, but love is often the last thing to be found in the relationship. It is more likely to be about selfish desires for personal pleasure.

David is drawn deeper into the web of his own making, by his request to see her. Soon he is in just that sort of relationship. Then with Bathsheba pregnant and her husband away at war he faces a problem. David tries some cover up measures – he quickly sends a message to his general, Joab, to have Uriah sent home to give a report. Uriah, the hero of this story arrives at the palace and after a brief interview with David is sent home for a rest (verse 8). Uriah the faithful servant, however, refuses this very welcome relief, and spends the night with the palace guards. Can you imagine the frustration of David when he discovers that Uriah didn't go home as he *contrasts* his adultery and Uriah's loyalty. Any soldier on campaign, whether he was away or home was not expected to enjoy the comforts of wife and home! You can feel David's sentiments when he asks Uriah, 'You have just returned after a long absence; why didn't you go home?'

David tries another ploy. He arranges for Uriah to eat with him and gets him drunk, hoping that in his drunken state he would find his way home and into bed with Bathsheba. Sometimes we try to cover up our wrong to someone by expressing kindness, but when that appears to fail it gives way to hatred and, in this case, desperation.

In this desperation David pens a letter to General Joab and arranges to have Uriah killed in battle. Uriah carries his own death warrant to the battlefield and meets his end in a scandalous attack. It appears that with very little remorse, after the official mourning period, Bathsheba joined David's harem and became his wife!

Again we see the tragic way a little temptation, and our response to it can bring a chain of events into action. The borrowing of a pen from work that soon becomes paper, paper clips, folders etc. The use of the telephone for private phone calls in work time. We would prefer to deny that these are stealing, but that is what they are! The initial lie to the wife about 'working late' is then followed by a string of subsequent lies.

The next thing in this sorry story, is the visit to David's court of a prophet by the name of Nathan with a story about sheep, a rich man and a poor man. Like the rest of us David listens, intently, to the 'story'. The trouble is David finds himself to be the villain of this devastating parable. Seeing himself in the story David in great remorse prostrates himself on the floor and refuses to eat anything for a week.

God caught up with David's sin. Sin very often brings its own judgement. In David's case God brought him to realise his own failings through a simple story. Bob remembers as a teenager of eighteen years, when riding his bike one evening, when God suddenly confronted him with a particular sin that he was continually giving in to. It was like a thunderbolt when he felt the full force of how God felt about what he was doing. He found himself underneath his bike saying, 'God, I'm really sorry, I won't do it again.' God never lets us off the hook; he loves us too much to do that. He gently, and sometimes more forcibly points out our failures in order that we might become better.

4

No cover up
Jesus

Jesus, the son of God, was no exception: even he faced the attacks of the evil tempter. Please read Luke 4:1–13.

Jesus's 'temptations' come immediately after his baptism. It was at his baptism in the river Jordan by John that he received a unique experience of his relationship with God his Father. As he came out of the water we read that 'heaven was opened, and the Holy Spirit came down upon him in bodily form like a dove. And a voice came from heaven, "You are my own dear Son. I am pleased with you".'

Immediately after this anointing Jesus is found in the desert! The contrast is enormous. So much so that three of the Gospels stress the closeness of the two events. Jesus came from a 'hilltop' experience of knowing that he was in his Father's will to a wilderness. The wilderness mentioned here in these verses, is probably what the Old Testament calls 'Jeshimon' which means 'The Devastation' – yellow sand, crumbling limestone and scattered shingle with hillside ridges running in all directions, warped, twisted and gnarled by the tremendous heat of the daytime sun and by night-time cold. Not exactly the best place for a Sunday afternoon picnic.

It was a depressing place and Jesus 'deliberately' went there to be *alone*.

Many people whom we know share our experience that after the 'hilltop' we are very quickly brought down to earth with a bump to face the harsh realities of life. We are rapidly brought into temptation – and the devil knows how to bring us down.

Jesus had chosen to be alone to seek God as to how he was going to launch his ministry. It was a crucial time for Jesus to make 'choices', and it was *not* made easier because he was the son of God. On the contrary because he didn't give way to the devil it was even harder for him. Let us briefly look at the three ways he was tempted. Remember that Jesus hasn't eaten for forty days, and the voice very clearly says, 'Order this stone to turn into bread'. The visual element is again powerful in Jesus's temptation. This desert was not like the Sahara, it was covered by lumps of limestone rock which looked very similar to the baked loaves of the day. Jesus was being asked to demonstrate who he was by the miraculous – using his powers to attract followers, but more than that, using his gifts simply to bring about material benefits. Jesus answers very clearly that he has not come to demonstrate God's kingdom by making people better off: 'Man cannot live on bread alone' (verse 4).

Again the devil, realising that Jesus is not easy prey to that line of tempting, tries a different tack. He takes Jesus to the highest mountain and shows him 'the kingdoms of the world ...'. He continues, 'I will give you all this power and wealth ... if you worship me' (verse 7). What a terrific temptation. 'Compromise, Jesus, don't set your standards so high.' The devil is suggesting that to compromise with evil will attract a lot more followers. We all find it difficult to follow someone who is continually good, and the devil is tempting Jesus to come down and be more realistic. Jesus retaliated very quickly, 'Worship the Lord your God and serve only him'.

The third temptation, whether real or imagined is perhaps the most eye-catching suggestion yet – the modern media would have had a field day! Jesus is taken to the highest point of the Jerusalem temple where there is a sheer drop of 450 feet (137 metres) into the Kidron Valley. Jesus was being recommended to throw himself down and become a 'sensationalist' of the first degree, to induce followers by dramatic acts of miraculous wonder. To do this would make him no better than many magicians of the day – a five-day wonder. Jesus rejected this path: 'Do not put the Lord your God to the test.'

For many years as a youngster and a teenager the thought kept coming to mind, that Jesus was very fortunate in only being tempted on those three occasions. Yes, they were difficult at the time. Obviously this was a very naive view, and far from the truth. We read in verse 13, 'When the devil finished tempting Jesus in *every way*, he left him for *a while*'.

In those forty days there were not just three temptations; with the intense heat of the day and the chilling nights, there would have been many times when Jesus would have wanted to throw in the towel. Jesus was tempted in 'every way' and the temptations were not limited to the time in the wilderness – they returned later in his ministry. Being completely God and completely man at the same time, did not remove Jesus from any temptations that we face. On the contrary, because he was God/man the pressure was even greater.

Jesus was fully human – he had a natural birth, grew up as other boys, ate food, was hungry, thirsty, tired, limited by time and space and knew what it was like to face the many inhumanities that today would warrant an investigation by Amnesty International. He expressed the human properties of mind, emotion and will: he needed to ask questions, showed love for his friends, anger, moral indignation and sorrow, he wept, showed compassion, and prepared to accept his Father's will. Because Jesus was God/man, he was more human than we are – sin had not tainted his humanity.

Jesus's continual temptation as a human being was necessary if he was to be able to help us today. The writer to the Hebrews makes it clear when he says, 'And now he can help those who are tempted, because he himself was tempted and suffered' (Hebrews 2:18). So I can pray with full confidence that all the troubles, trials and temptations that I face now, have already been experienced in part by Jesus. Therefore Jesus is not God in the sky sitting on a throne with little or no sympathy; on the contrary he is One who can 'feel sympathy for our weaknesses ... who was tempted in every way that we are, but did not sin' (Hebrews 4:15). If we do not understand this we shall find it harder to understand the subject of forgiveness and God's strength to overcome our temptations.

The long silence

At the end of time, billions of people were scattered on a great plain before God's Throne.

Most shrank back from the brilliant light before them. But some groups near the front talked heatedly – not with cringing shame, but with belligerence.

'Can God judge us? How can he know about suffering?' snapped a pert young brunette. She ripped open a sleeve to reveal a tattooed number from a Nazi concentration camp. 'I've endured terror ... beatings ... torture ... death!'

In another group a negro boy lowered his collar. 'What about this?' he demanded, showing an ugly rope burn. 'Lynched for no crime but being black!'

In another crowd, a pregnant schoolgirl with sullen eyes. 'Why should I suffer?' she murmered. 'It wasn't my fault.' Far out across the plain were hundreds of such groups. Each had a complaint against God for the evil and suffering he permitted in his world.

How lucky God was to live in heaven where all was sweetness and light, where there was no weeping or fear, no hunger or hatred.

What did God know of all that man had been forced to endure in this world? For God leads a pretty sheltered life, they said.

So each of these groups sent forth their leader, chosen because he had suffered the most. A Jew, a Negro, a person from Hiroshima, a horribly deformed arthritic, a thalidomide child.

In the centre of the plain they consulted with each other. At last they were ready to present their case. It was rather clever.

Before God could be qualified to be their judge, he must endure what they had endured. Their decision was that God should be sentenced to live on earth – as a man!

Let him be born a Jew. Let the legitimacy of his birth be doubted. Give him a work so difficult that even his family will think him out of his mind when he tries to do it. Let him be betrayed by his closest friends. Let him face false charges, be tried by a prejudiced jury and convicted by a cowardly judge. Let him be tortured.

At the last, let him see what it means to be terribly alone. Then let him die. Let him die so that there can be no doubt he died. Let there be a great host of witnesses to verify it.

As each leader announced his portion of the sentence loud murmurs of approval went up from the throng of people assembled.

When the last had finished pronouncing sentence there was a long silence. No one uttered another word. No one moved. For suddenly all knew that God had already served his sentence.

Anon.

5

Why temptation?

Temptation seems always to be with us

We can't remember when we were first 'tempted'. It just seems that we always have been. Even now as we look at young children they don't seem to have any problems finding ways of getting up to mischief. They, unlike us, haven't been schooled in: how to 'cheat' and get away with it; how to 'borrow' something from someone else and 'forget' to give it back, or how to 'lie' (or not tell the whole truth) convincingly. Sadly the ability to do all these things is not something that is taught or even learned; it is inbred into each one of us. Some might say, 'Well, it was his background, his environment that made him act that way.' Like most statements of that nature this contains an element of truth. Obviously our parents' reactions to the way we act and think affect us, as do school and friends. However, irrespective of our background, environment, social status etc. there is still the choice of 'right' and 'wrong'. The choice is an individual one and cannot be blamed onto someone else or society as a whole. Our choice may become heavily biassed in one direction or another by our background; our consciences (something which we are going to look at later) can become hardened but the choice is still ours, and judgements in a court of law reflect that.

Why Doesn't God ... eliminate the devil? That way he could let us off the hook – no tempter, no temptation, no sin! If God had done that then Adam and Eve wouldn't have made the first mistake that we read about in the Bible (Genesis 3) of taking fruit from the tree that they were told explicitly that they shouldn't. In fact why did God put the tree there in the first place?

Why Doesn't God ... direct our eyes away from temptation? For example a shopper in your local supermarket inadvertently drops a £20 note from a large roll in his hand as he passes some money to the cashier. What do you do? He appears not to have noticed, nor has anybody else – a gift for you? Why doesn't God turn our heads away, distract us and suggest that we look at a flower!! It almost seems that God has made us that way – to be tempted – then gets upset when we give in to temptation. It seems unfair.

Why Doesn't God ... dampen our passions? God could, if he wanted, put that bit of us right. If he is all powerful, that would be no problem – change those biases within us and make us less open to temptation.

So why doesn't God make it easier for us?

Temptations put a check on our loyalty to him. God tested Abraham by seemingly asking him to sacrifice his only son Isaac (Genesis 22:1–14). Not only would this be a personal tragedy it would be sacrificing, as far as Abraham knew, the possibility of ever having his family name continue through his son. Abraham's temptation to believe that he had got it badly wrong or that God had got it badly wrong must have torn him from head to toe. He passed the test, however, and his actions demonstrated that he was someone who loved his God.

Sometimes our loyalty is challenged; do we go the way of our friends or the way of God. 'That' party where you know that the end result is to get 'stoned' or the evening with friends where you know that you will end up 'gossiping about others'.

God's way is never easy, but temptations certainly act as a magnifying glass to show us and God how loyal we really are.

Temptations build our character. It has been said that if you walk along a path that has no obstacles, it probably doesn't lead anywhere. Without temptations our characters would be weak and lifeless. An athlete preparing for a race, can't afford any flabbiness or excess weight. He has to train and exercise his body in every conceivable way to teach it to act properly on the track and attain the most efficiency from it in order to win the race. Paul writes this to the Philippian church: 'I do not claim that I have already succeeded or have already become perfect. I keep striving to win the prize for which Christ Jesus has already won me to himself. Of course, my brothers, I really do not think that I have already won it; the one thing I do, however, is to forget what is behind me and do my best to reach what is ahead. So I run straight towards the goal in order to win the prize, which is God's call through Christ Jesus to the life above' (Philippians 3:12–14). As Christians, every time we resist a temptation we are 'body building': we are in the business of producing a personality and character that expresses Christ. We will be encouraged by the realisation that we are being drawn closer to, and becoming better followers of, Jesus.

The writer to the Romans makes this clear: 'We also boast of our troubles because we know that trouble produces endurance, endurance brings God's approval, and his approval creates hope' (Romans 5:3,4).

Paul makes no bones about it. If you want to succeed as a Christian then you must patiently endure all the temptations and trials that you face. It is like 'the weights' to the body builders! If you want to become a mature Christian and receive God's approval then 'stick in' with the temptations.

He gets so excited that he says, he is prepared to 'boast' about his testings because, he knows that they produce 'patient endurance' and that creates God's approval of his new and changing character. He is saying (almost) that he looks forward to trials and temptations because he knows that they will help him to grow in the Christian life.

Bob remembers at the age of twenty-three, being asked to lead an overland coach trip to Russia (and back!) for three weeks with forty-four students. Before that his only experience had been a trip across the Irish Sea (at the age of twelve) to see his ageing grandmother. With a brand new passport and with no experience of any languages or foreign customs, Bob travelled with the party through France, Belgium, Holland, West Germany, East Germany, Poland and Russia to Moscow. Every evening they camped at a new campsite and Bob had to organise the erection of the tents, cooking, and so on. He was interrogated on the Russian border and the army trailer that they were towing with all their camping gear and supplies fell off as they were travelling along. (The coach went on for twenty-five miles before they realised!) Bob was threatened with immediate imprisonment for allowing this to happen. Close to exhaustion, he had to keep the morale of the party going as well as present numerous forms to impatient customs officials. In all of that, however, his faith in God grew during that three weeks of his life in a way that he has never since experienced over such a short period.

Testing of our characters through trials and temptations can only produce a greater depth of faith.

Temptations show us our weaknesses. In a peculiar kind of way, when we do give in to a temptation, if we stop to realise it, it just shows us how weak we really are. Paul appreciates this when he writes to the Corinthian church: 'I am content ... for when I am weak, then I am strong' (2 Corinthians 12:10).

New year resolutions not to argue with parents, brothers, sisters, not to smoke, to tell the whole truth, all seem to go by the board within a few hours or a few days. Promises to God that we won't allow anything to distract us from our prayer and Bible-reading often end with us saying sorry to God yet again for failing him.

We're not recommending that just because you give in you should give up. God in his mercy, wants to strike at the very core of our attitudes and motives to help us not only face our weaknesses but to recognise that we need his strength and power.

It is only when we are weak and realise it that God can help us to resist temptation. Temptations help us to recognise that we need God more than we are prepared to admit.

6
The temptation process

How do we know right from wrong?

Alan tells his boss Mark that he was as 'sick as a dog' the day before and therefore didn't feel up to work. Mark being a trusting character accepts Alan's story and after a few sympathetic remarks returns to his office. As soon as Mark is out of earshot, Alan boasts that 'yesterday' he had had the opportunity to go down to the coast with a guy who had just bought the latest souped-up Porsche. By lunchtime the Porsche had turned into a Rolls-Royce and the coast had turned to a gaming club in the city.

Alan could be termed a compulsive 'liar'. He perhaps doesn't even 'feel' tempted to lie or not to, he just does it. We may say it just becomes second nature to him. His conscience doesn't prompt him to reconsider his action – it just happens. It does not mean, however, that when Alan sees a watch that he likes at the local jewellers, he just picks it up and pockets it without paying. Oh, no. Alan may have very strong views about stealing and what should be done to those people who do those kind of things ... 'Do what they do in those Arab countries, cut their hands off!'

Temptation can only be real to a person if he or she has moral views about a particular action or thought in the first place. If Alan has no moral opinion that lying is wrong then there is very little or no temptation. However Alan may change his mind about lying if someone deliberately tries to deceive him ... in fact he may have very strong views!

Many people make their decision as to what is right or wrong by what they have been taught by their parents or their friends. Perhaps 'taught' is too strong a word because most of us follow by example. For instance, a parent may clout a teenager round the ear for swearing, and yet the words used were learnt by hearing his parents using them. 'Do as I say, not as I do!' Then there are the friends who have other ideas about their behaviour code. This may be to get away with what you can while you can. The Bible has its suggestions on the way we should live; for many people, if only in a rather vague way, some parts of the Bible are part of their background. For example, the Ten Commandments.

One	Worship only God
Two	Don't make idols for yourself
Three	Do not blaspheme
Four	Keep the Sabbath holy
Five	Respect your mother and father
Six	Do not commit murder
Seven	Do not commit adultery
Eight	Do not steal
Nine	Do not lie
Ten	Do not be jealous about what some-body else has (Exodus 20:1–17)

Many are brought up to do good, be kind and try to keep the commandments, and not to do 'unto other people what they wouldn't like done to them'. They have to grapple with all the 'Do's and Don'ts' to decide what is right or wrong for them. Their temptations to do wrong are based on what they conceive to be right.

For the Christian, however, what is right and wrong is not just a question of numerous influences and suggestions upon us. First of all there are the Ten Commandments to help us judge the rightness of our actions. For the Christian these are much more than some vague set of rules – they are a clear summary of what God expects from his people. 'Should I lie?' Answer, 'No'. 'Should I say when I can't think of any other phrase to use: 'Oh, Jesus Christ!' Answer, 'No'. The commandments say we shouldn't lie (number Nine) and we shouldn't blaspheme, or use God's name in a derogatory way (number Three). It is that simple, but that simplicity is very often a stumbling block for many of us, as we can easily try to justify our proposed actions to do what 'we' want to do.

The Ten Commandments are often called 'absolutes', which means that they can stand as God's set of rules for everybody, at any time, and in any place. For the Christian they are one of the clearest and most direct summaries of what God expects, but throughout the Bible there is teaching as to how we should behave.

God's commandments are spelt out in the life and teachings of Jesus. He is our walking example of all that God wants us to be. His love, kindness, gentleness, honesty and justice are to be models for us, his teaching, in the Sermon on the Mount for instance, takes us beyond simple obedience to the letter of the Commandments and challenges us about our attitudes.

Everyone has an inbuilt sense of right and wrong – we call it conscience, the 'voice' that stops and makes us think, but it can only be effective if it is given over to God's thinking. When we become Christians our conscience becomes sharper, more alert and better informed. The Holy Spirit who is given to us by God when we become Christians wants to fill our lives with all that is good and right and to give us God's very best. Therefore the Holy Spirit within us will certainly want to influence our actions very quickly and he will use our conscience in a new way to help us to decide between what is good and bad, right and wrong.

It must be realised, however, that at this point temptation becomes even stronger. Before someone becomes a Christian the devil considers a person belonging to his 'party' anyway ... the conscience has been dulled and the individual feels no accountability until whatever he or she does comes into conflict with the 'law'. As a Christian it is completely the reverse. The Christian is continually striving to serve God; he or she is therefore a number one candidate for temptation, because the devil wants to make things tough.

The process of temptation

St. Augustine (354–430) had a marvellous insight into the development of temptation and declared that the thought follows the look; delight comes after the thought; and consent after delight. Augustine was no angel before his conversion to Christianity; he wrote, 'I felt that I was still enslaved by my sins and in misery I kept crying …' Then he opened a book containing Paul's letters … 'and in silence I read the first passage on which my eyes fell: "No orgies or drunkenness, no immorality or indecency, no fighting or jealousy".' Confronted by these words Augustine made his decision to become a follower of Jesus. Augustine speaks from experience. He sees temptation following the path shown in this diagram.

LOOK ⇨ THOUGHT ⇨ DELIGHT ⇨ CONSENT

TEMPTATION   SIN

The 'looking' is not 'sin', even the initial 'thought' that may develop from the look is not 'sin', but to entertain that thought consciously and deliberately for more than a few moments can lead us into sin. Here is a very simple example. While out driving one afternoon we turn into a road where there are beautiful large houses one after another, after another, after another ... We 'look', and then the 'thought' processes come into action where we imagine ourselves and our two daughters living in this 'palace'. So far so good, until our thinking moves us, not only wishing that we had a house like that, but also feeling very jealous about those who were very fortunate ('bet they inherited it') to be ('I expect they don't have to keep the garden tidy') living ('lounging around doing nothing but being served with cold drinks around the swimming pool all day') there ('they don't deserve it, it's not fair').

Allowing our 'thoughts' to work overtime can lead us into a position of sinning against God. Let's take a look at another Christian who also said much to help us with temptation. St. Bernard (1090–1153) had a very different start from Augustine. At the age of twenty-one he entered a monastery and turned his back on the world and its comforts. He lived a life of prayer and self-denial during which he made this gloomy statement:

'The thought which is not rejected produces pleasure.
Pleasure leads to consent.
Consent to action.
Action to habit.
Habit to a kind of necessity.
And necessity to eternal death.'

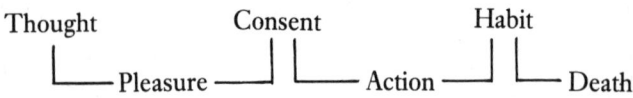

Bernard takes Augustine's thinking further. 'Actions' are not needed for sin to take place. Entertaining a 'thought' that our conscience says 'no' to becomes sin. Jesus makes this very clear when he is talking about a man looking at a woman, '... anyone who looks at a woman and wants to possess her is guilty of committing adultery with her in his heart' (Matthew 5:28). This is not, however, justification for carrying through the action just because you thought of it anyway. Just because you have given in to sin by the 'thought' it does not mean you should harm someone else by carrying your 'thought' into 'action'.

Habits

When we give way in our temptation, allowing the thoughts to remain and lead us into actions, it immediately makes it easier for next time. That's the subtlety of our mind, 'Well I did it that time, and right or wrong, there's no harm in doing it again.'

During the period from 1965 to 1970 rational and responsible behaviour was frowned upon by many in exchange for the quest of 'experience'. These were the times of 'free love' (sex), drugs and the 'flower power'. There were those who wanted to try 'hash' (cannabis) just *once* for the 'experience'. The once became twice, three times and on and on, to where 'hash' became boring. So naturally the temptation to 'inject' just *once*, just for 'kicks', to see what that was like, became the start of another slippery slope.

God must be very sad, as he watches the way we allow our temptations to become habits. There is a Spanish proverb that says, 'Habits are first cobwebs, then cables'. Have you ever watched a fly caught in a cobweb? He appears to be so large in comparison to each of the little threads yet the more he moves, the more ensnared he becomes.

There is a very revealing phrase that the writer to the Romans repeats as he talks about God's anger for the evil that is committed: '... God has given them over ...' (Romans

1:24,26). It would be useful to read verses 18–32 of this chapter in Romans about actions which lead to natural judgement and punishment. To quote just a small section, 'And so God has given those people over to do the filthy things their hearts desire, and they do shameful things with each other. They exchange the truth about God for a lie, they worship and serve what God has created instead of the Creator himself ...' (verses 24–25).

Body movement

Certain foods and drinks, tiredness and clothing can stimulate or suppress many of our thoughts and actions which bring temptation to us. For example, drinking quantities of coffee without food may well make us touchy and agitated. One of our daughters reacts in a similar way to a particular 'colouring additive' in one of the cordials. Alcohol is an obvious problem area. What one person may find a reasonable drinking level involving no loss of control may be well over the top for the next person.

For the technically minded, there is a more detailed account on this subject in the Appendix under the same title.

The temptation process can be compared to angling. The bait is dropped alongside of us; it looks very inviting, particularly as it has been found close by and within the environment that is known (the water). However the fish rarely sees the hook, the hidden danger, or the consequence of accepting the bait. Sin occurs, then, when we yield to the bait and bite the bait. Sin results in tragic consequences – and we can end up 'hooked and fried'.

7

What happens if I give in to temptation?

First the bad news

Adam and Eve, David and Bathsheba, John Smith (he has to get a mention somewhere), you and I, all suffer from the same dreaded disease ... SIN. From the very moment Adam and Eve disobeyed God by taking the fruit from the tree, they not only found that they knew about sin, they also brought every person into a similar state. Our children have never had lessons in how to lie, or fight with one another. We have not sat them down in a chair and had a teaching session on how to 'answer back' or to 'pull the wool over our eyes' and get away with it. They do it quite *naturally*, and that sadly is the key; it comes 'naturally' to all of us. It is basic human nature. We are not, as some people would say, by 'nature' good; on the contrary we are continually being tempted to do wrong and we don't need much assistance. The Bible makes it very clear, '... everyone has sinned and is far away from God's saving presence' (Romans 3:23). When we give in to temptation and knowingly do wrong we sin, we disobey God and deserve to be punished.

It is the devil's lie to us as it was to Eve and Adam, that just one fall, one little sin, does not really matter; 'You can recover,' he tells us. Then once we have given in to that temptation and have sinned, the devil very cleverly tells us that it is now hopeless, and – and here is the crunch – there is no need to attempt to rise.

When we realise that we have failed and have let God down we begin to feel guilt and shame. Psychiatrists will tell you, that guilt is one of the most common reasons for their professional help being sought. Guilt makes you feel like a second class citizen; it can make you rehearse your sin or sins in vivid detail. Guilt can make you end up feeling and acting like driving a car with the brake on. Look at some of the effects of guilt in our chart.

POTENTIAL EFFECTS OF GUILT

Depression: Continually moody, with feelings of hopelessness and worthlessness.

Aggression: Seeing our own failures, there comes a tendency to pick up the same failures in others.

Apathy and Indifference: As feelings are suppressed and stifled, we cease to care and lose interest.

Anger: Striking out at others because we feel trapped by blame.

Perfectionism: Feeling guilty we try even harder to create an ideal world around us and to be perfectionists in what we do.

Self-degradation: Continually turning our guilt feelings inward hoping that when we make a negative comment about ourselves someone will contradict us, thus taking the pressure off a bit.

Guilt can also bring physical illness. Our minds, burdened with carrying the weight of our guilt, use far more of our energy, in the end causing our bodies to malfunction at some point. Susan is a sincere Christian and wants to be obedient to God. At college she met Pete and finding a mutual attraction she naturally began spending a great deal of time with him. As a result she failed her finals. As she begins to think it through, it is as though a big cloud surrounds her. She begins to blame Pete for her failure, and to look for a job; but she feels that she has failed already wth her examinations and she believes that she will let her employers down even if she could find work. Finding herself living at home once again she picks on her younger brother who is preparing for his 'A' levels. 'He's not working hard enough,' she tells her mother, 'he's always out with his friends.' Susan can't pray any more – she feels she's not good enough. She becomes moody and can find no way out of this 'smog'. Susan is seen by her doctor and found to be 'depressed'. Tablets are prescribed and the long struggle begins to fight her way out. Susan talks about feeling that she is travelling a long dark tunnel. Friends tells her that she will soon see light at the end of it. Susan, however, says that with all her luck she will just see an express train coming towards her!

A sad story, but only too true. Guilt is not the only reason for depression, but it is one of the more common.

Sin often brings its own natural judgements, as well. These may be physical or emotional; they may affect our relationships with others.

Sleeping around, casual affairs can bring their own judgement. Emotions that need healing and once healed, can still leave scars and unwanted pregnancies; although the 'pill' and abortion have taken away the latter threat. Venereal disease is still rampant and appears to bring God's natural judgement. Sadly children born to those with some forms of venereal disease can be adversely affected. AIDS (Acquired Immune Deficiency Syndrome) now widespread in the United States is a disease which seems to be chiefly transmitted through homosexual activity, but appears also to be occurring through normal heterosexual relationships.

Alcohol abuse, condemned (like casual sexual relationships) in the Bible leads to sad individuals who lose the respect of others and finally their own personality gives way to the bottle.

Obesity and stress brought on by greed can lead to heart attacks, strokes, and ulcers.

In much modern psychiatry, there is the view that it is important to open up the dark areas of a person's mind ... the things that happened in a person's childhood, to see how this has affected them and brought them to this stage in life. This can be very helpful but unless the guilt can be effectively dealt with we are back to square one – or even further back.

And now the good news

Jesus Christ, however, came to reveal all our sin and at the same time forgive us completely and remove the cloud that cripples our emotions and our bodies. Jesus is the Light (John 8:12) and wants to penetrate into every dark corner of our lives to heal and bring about a completeness, to make us more 'human'.

In his book, *God was in Christ*, D M Baillie gives us a picture which I have adapted a little. He asks us to imagine that a number of us are standing around in a circle looking outwards. In the centre of the circle, however, is a brilliant light. Anyone in the circle looking out, would see only a shadow of themselves, plus a shadow of other people close to them. The shadows are not the real 'us', but a shadow of their potential. If we then turned 90° to the right so that we are neither facing the light nor the darkness, we would be in a position to make a choice – the light or the darkness. The light that is unknown perhaps to the darkness of our past that we are only too familiar with. Not only that, the light being so intense begins to open up the dark areas which we may not be prepared to face. The choice is ours.

If we do make the choice to turn another 90° into the light, we can not only see the real 'me' but also the real 'me' of others. I no longer see the dark shadow; I see them in the light, I see them through Christ's eyes.

Christ does not want us to remain guilty. Yes, we have failed God by giving in to temptation. Yes, we have therefore rebelled against him. No, we don't deserve forgiveness. Yes, we may fail him again *but* we read very clearly in the Bible that Christ has set us free from the guilt of our sins: 'And with joy give thanks to the Father, who has made you fit to have your share of what God has reserved for his people in the kingdom of light. He rescued us from the power of darkness and brought us safe into the kingdom of his dear Son, by whom we are set free, that is, our sins are forgiven' (Colossians 1:12–14).

When Jesus Christ cried out on the cross 'It is finished!' he had taken the punishment for our sins upon himself in his death. The words he used in the Greek were also used in financial transactions to mean 'The debt is fully paid'. It's like taking a bill along to pay it, and then as we pass over our money, the stamp comes down on the bill 'PAID'. Christ has completely and utterly cancelled and forgotten our sin – all he asks of us is that we are sorry, that we determine to turn away from our sin and that we accept his forgiveness. It's like pushing the 'cancel' button on a calculator; the screen clears and we start afresh. Remember, we don't deserve forgiveness, which shows how great God's love and mercy are.

A mother once approached Napoleon seeking a pardon for her son. The Emperor replied that the young man had committed a certain offence twice and justice demanded death.

'But I don't ask for justice,' the mother explained. 'I plead for mercy.'

'But your son does not deserve mercy,' Napoleon replied.

'Sir,' the woman cried, 'it would not be mercy if he deserved it, and mercy is all I ask for.'

'Well then,' the Emperor said, 'I will have mercy'. And he spared her son.

We cannot separate the teachings of Jesus on this subject of forgiveness from his requirements on forgiving others.

The Lord's prayer, which Jesus taught his disciples, has at its core, the truth that forgiveness from God, comes through forgiving others: 'And forgive us our sins, as we forgive those that sin against us'. (Prayer Book, Matthew 6:12).

In Matthew 18:21–35 we read of Peter, one of Jesus's closest disciples working out his understanding of forgiveness. Peter had asked Jesus how many times should he forgive someone, and then typically made a suggestion – 'Seven times?'

In fact he had been very generous, as according to Jewish tradition you only had to forgive someone three times. Peter had multiplied by two and added one for luck! He was good at counting fish.

Jesus then takes Peter's generosity and multiplies it, to show how endless our forgiveness for others should be. Jesus tells a parable of the 'Unforgiving Servant'.

The contrast between the two debts is in the extreme. A

ruler (king) forgave his servant a debt of 10,000 talents. A 'talent' in this text is equivalent to a person's wage for *fifteen years*!

The king's servant would not forgive his own servant of just 100 denarii. A 'denarius' would be the payment for *one day's* labour.

By way of comparison let us say the servant owed his king £1,000,000 and was let off the debt. He then refused to forgive and forget his own servant's debt of £2!

Forgiveness then is ours. Freedom from sin and guilt, however, is always available from God, but never from the devil. He contests every step of the way to prevent us believing and accepting God's forgiveness. The devil will want to confuse us. He will keep prodding us and making us ask, 'How can we be forgiven?' Ignore him and accept by simple faith that you are now a child of Light and therefore forgiven. Remember that you are not alone. As Christians we are given the Holy Spirit to encourage and help us every moment of the day (Ephesians 5:18). More of this in the next chapter.

Convinced of your forgiveness? We hope so. A plate of well-prepared and appetising food is placed before a hungry man. He sits for the next hour looking at it, refusing to taste it! Ridiculous, of course, but no more ridiculous than failing to accept the forgiveness that Christ can give us. It's there for the taking!

8

How do I stop giving in to temptation?

How do I stop giving in to temptation? That is the crucial question; and to answer it is to provide one of the keys to growing as a Christian.

We could, we suppose, do what one celebrated hermit did until his death in AD 459. Simeon Stylites lived on a pillar of rock for thirty years; his only contact with the rest of the human race was having food and drink passed up to him! Even there, however, he would have faced temptation. Or perhaps not wishing to go to this extreme, we might take religious orders and live in a convent or monastery for the rest of our lives. Or maybe find a desert island to spend the rest of our days.

Run from it

If a ten ton lorry is hurtling towards me, if I haven't frozen with fear, I would throw myself out of its path. Common-sense suggests that as the most logical course. Not that I stop to discuss the validity of my logic, or consider the implications of any lack of action. I just run!

Joseph had been sold into slavery by his jealous brothers. He ended up as master in charge of Potiphar's house.

Potiphar was the captain of the palace guard responsible for palace security for the king. Joseph had a problem; Potiphar's wife fancied him. He persistently refused her advances and requests to share her bed until one day, his luck ran out (Genesis 39:1–23). While all the servants were out, Potiphar's wife '... caught him by his robe and said, "Come to bed with me". But he escaped and ran outside leaving his robe in her hand' (verses 12,13). In her frustration and annoyance she claimed that Joseph had tried to rape her, but her screams had prevented the attack and he fled leaving the robe in her hand. Joseph was thrown into prison ...

Joseph 'ran' from the temptation. The more we entertain the temptation the harder it is to overcome.

If you have problems do you run from the things that stimulate your temptation? Bob once agreed to speak to someone who was constantly tempted to buy pornographic magazines. Every day on his way home from work, he would just stop at a magazine shop and buy another one. One simple step to minimise his temptation was to come home a different way, so that he could avoid that particular shop.

That was the first step, but it was the most important. Take the person who couldn't stop buying clothes from one of those catalogues where you choose your goods and send off for them. Not only was the wardrobe becoming like the 'royals' but the bills were adding up. Again a very simple step but the most important was to destroy the catalogue. Bob will now no longer turn to page three of a certain national newspaper. To avoid the temptation he avoids the place where temptation is found.

Face up to it

Ask yourself the question: is what I am about to watch (television or cinema) going to be helpful to me, or are my thoughts going to be taken in a direction that I, as a Christian don't want to go along? Ask the same question about the things you hear and the things you read. Face up to honest answers and take action.

We both have a problem with the television. We put it on for a particular programme and we find ourselves glued to it a long while after we had really intended. We end up at the end of the late films saying to each other 'What a wasted evening, why did we allow ourselves to do that again?'

If you play around with something that you know will lead you into sin, you will end up tolerating it. 'It's not that bad after all,' you may convince yourself, but you are probably just lowering your standards to accommodate your lowered level of behaviour. Be practical. If you're serious about facing up to your temptations make a list of them and use the 'Factors' below to help you.

The 'Yes' Factor

Coming out on top when we face temptation is not a matter of saying 'No', it is a matter of saying 'Yes'. Jesus did not say 'No' to bread, he did say 'Yes' to the bread of heaven. He did not say 'No' to political messiahship, he said 'Yes' to messiahship which was more than political and social. He did not say 'No' to worshipping Satan, he said 'Yes' to worshipping God. You will find that in every temptation and in every situation there is something corresponding to the negative which is very positive. You do not say 'No' to doing your homework, you say 'Yes' to paying a visit to the library for two hours on your way home from school. You do not say in the first place 'No' to flirting with your secretary, you say 'Yes' to the woman who washes your dirty underwear several times a week. Instead of saying 'No' to the television programme you don't really want to watch, you say 'Yes' to picking up a book.

Study this. Think about it. If you merely say 'No', that still leaves your life in a vacuum and makes you a negative, empty person. To say 'Yes' to that which is positive makes you a positive servant of God. A person full of the Holy Spirit will always be positive.
BE PRACTICAL.

The 'Run' Factor

We have already seen that, like Joseph, we mustn't stay around when the temptation is strongest. On the contrary, we run. Dag Hammarskjold, one-time General Secretary of the United Nations, has said, 'You can't play with the animal in you without becoming wholly animal, play with falsehood without forfeiting your right to truth, play with cruelty without losing your sensitivity of mind. He who wants to keep his garden tidy doesn't reserve a plot for weeds.' If your temptation is to continually eat then arrange your diary for the week so that you are not alone enough to eat yourself out of house and home.
BE PRACTICAL.

The 'Person' Factor

In the survey that we did before writing this book, many people were helped by sharing their problems. It's good to be able to tell someone else not only so that they can advise but so that they can check up on our progress (or otherwise). Have someone you trust keep their eye on you; someone who will support you, encourage you, pray for you, someone you will not 'answer' back, but whose comments you will respect. BE PRACTICAL.

There is a Chinese Proverb that says, 'You can't stop birds flying overhead, but you can stop them nesting in your hair'.

Where Do I Get Help?

Prayer 'How glib can you get,' we can hear you saying. 'I've tried that but it doesn't seem to help.'

Praying over your temptation is only going to work if you are really serious about getting it sorted out. It is like dancing – if the partners fail to keep in step a lot of pain and bruises result. God wants us to dance in step with him. It is only if we follow his lead and believe that he wants to help us more than we can ever imagine, that we begin to agree with his timing.

Paul writes to the Corinthian church saying this: 'Every test (temptation) that you have experienced is the kind that normally comes to people. But God keeps his promise, and he will not allow you to be tested beyond your power to remain firm; at the time you are put to the test, he will give you the strength to endure it, and so provide you with a way out' (1 Corinthians 10:13). Do you get the picture? As we step with God, he is allowing these temptations, but at the same time he will give us the strength to endure them. As you pray to God about your temptations, pray with that in mind.

In some famous verses in Galatians 5:22,23, we read that one of the things that God's Spirit gives to all of us (if we readily accept it) is *self-control*. As Christians, potentially within us we *have* (not in the future or only sometimes) self-control – God's given inner strength. When you pray then don't ask God for his strength and power to overcome (he has given that), but rather that you might know what practical steps to take to avoid the temptation. Prayer is powerful and it is one of the strongest weapons we have in our fight against the Devil. Let us read from a *Letter From Down Under* written from one devil to another:

My Dear Brimstone,

My master Lucifer has commanded me to jot you a memo concerning some of our enemy's followers up on earth – those who are called Christians. He is worried that there are small pockets of them who are actually praying: this, as you know, is very dangerous for us as it is their greatest weapon, and we have no defences when they call to Almighty God. What I want you to do is to stop it. If you fail in this mission Lucifer has promised that both you and I will never be the same again – so for Hell's sake, Brimstone, do not fail me!

You should not find it too difficult – many who call themselves Christians only pray when they are personally in trouble: do not bother with that sort – they belong to us already! The ones to attack are those who spend time alone and in small groups praising God and praying hard for others as well as themselves, and whose lives are full of love.

Disrupt their praying, sow doubts in their minds, make them feel so tired that all they can do is flop in front of their TVs, make them talk about prayer instead of actually praying, make them argue about it when God delays his answer, get people to interrupt their prayer groups with silly comments – you know the sort of thing. SUCCEED!

Yours, Rt. Dishon. Sulphur.
Minister of Infernal Affairs.

The Bible

The devil hates the Bible. Why? Because it is God's word to us. The last thing the devil wants, is for us to know what God thinks about our 'sin'. Like prayer however, it is a powerful weapon. Jesus, when he was being tempted, quoted scripture in reply (Matthew 4:1–11):

The Devil: 'If you are God's Son, order these stones to turn into bread'.
Jesus: The scripture says, 'Man cannot live on bread alone, but needs every word that God speaks'. (Deuteronomy 8:3)
The Devil: 'If you are God's Son, throw yourself down from the temple pinnacle'.
Jesus: But the scripture also says, 'Do not put the Lord your God to the test'. (Deuteronomy 6:16)
The Devil: 'All this I will give you, if you kneel down and worship me'.
Jesus: The scripture says 'Worship the Lord your God and serve only him!' (Deuteronomy 6:13)

If Jesus, the Son of God, feels that quoting scripture at the devil is helpful, then so should we. We should read, read and read the Bible as much as we can so that we may know how to reply to the devil when he tempts us. We may not be able to quote chapter and verse, but we may well be able to recall an incident in the life of one of God's servants in the Old Testament or a statement by Jesus or Paul. We need to know what the Bible teaches on certain issues. If we are like a sponge in our reading of the Bible then when we are prodded by the devil into sin, what comes out will be what went in. Naturally the devil will try to stop us reading our Bibles at all costs – he will try every conceivable way to get us to put our Bible down, or better still not to pick it up!

Another 'Letter from down under':

My Dear Brimstone,

My master Lucifer has another job for you, following our recent successes in preventing our enemies' activities from flourishing.

He has noticed among those who call themselves Christians that many more these days seem to be spending time learning about their faith by reading their Bibles. This must stop!

What he commands you to do is first of all to do anything you can to stop them reading this Life Book on their own: keep them asleep in the mornings, or get someone to phone them up just when they have settled down to read it.

If they do decide to read it, try to get them to think of all the tricky and obscure passages instead of the solid ones which will help their faith grow. Get them to read an old-fashioned version where the language will be beautiful but the meaning totally hidden. If they begin to go to a Bible Study Group, make them feel too tired that night to go out. Make them afraid to ask for a copy of the Bible Reading Notes so many are using and finding so helpful.

Brimstone, once Christians know their God's mind from reading their Bibles, they are very dangerous to us: they will know right from wrong, how to stay in their God's plan, how to relate to people, how to witness, how to pray and so on! I do not need to say more! If you do not stop this powerful Bible reading, Lucifer has things in mind for you! Do not fail or your life will not be worth living at all!

Yours Faithlessly,

Rt. Dishon. Sulphur.
Minister of Infernal Affairs.

Try to memorise one verse of the Bible a week. Write it out on a card and keep it with you so that you can look at it occasionally.

One verse that has meant a lot to us is Philippians 4:13: 'I have the strength to face all conditions by the power that Christ gives me'. When we are up against it, as a family and tempted to take the easy way out, that verse stands as God's promise to us. This is another real problem for the devil, for if Christians believe the Bible and accept the promises it makes, the devil has to run. Your Bible is the equivalent of a gunslinger's six-shooter – USE IT!

Friends – Family – Minister

God has put us in families for our security and natural friendship and love. When we became Christians we joined God's worldwide family. The church is not always perfect, but we should not condemn it since God has put us in it for a purpose. Someone has said, 'The church is a hospital for sinners, not a rest home for saints'. Within the church, as God's family, therefore, we should allow ourselves to be open to other 'family' members who will share our problems and temptations; we should be ready to seek the necessary help. Sometimes it can be the minister, at other times close friends, on other occasions it may be helpful to speak to a complete stranger whom we will never see again until we get to heaven!

The devil wants to confuse you, to make you feel that you are the only miserable Christian in the whole world who has failed God. The last thing the devil wants you to do is to talk to anyone about it, and so he puts suggestions into our minds: 'What would they think?' 'You did that!' 'Your mind works that way.' Can you hear it? Talk it through with someone you can trust. To your surprise you may find that they have had the same problem. Even if they haven't they will have failed in other areas and will know how you feel. But beware of talking to everybody, and remember that the first person who appears with a listening ear may not be the right one to talk to.

Remember that you are part of God's family and God wants to change you. But he will not force change upon you. Call sin, sin! That's positive, because you are recognising your condition and that offers hope – do that and you're nine-tenths of the way there. Sharing your problem enables others to show you God's views in the Bible, and gives them the privilege of praying for you.

9
Putting it together

A Frenchman who became a naturalised Englishman was asked what difference it had made. He thought for a moment and then said, 'Last year Waterloo was a defeat, but now it's a victory'.

That should be our Christian experience so far as temptation is concerned. We are now on the winning side. Before we became a Christian, not only did we have to face temptation alone and try to find a solution within ourselves but the idea of 'victory' was a dream.

As Christians we cannot opt out of the 'temptation scene'. On the contrary it becomes our greatest test of faith and is the opportunity to help us grow into greater maturity. But this temptation does not come from God. 'If a person is tempted by such trials, he must not say, "This temptation comes from God." For God cannot be tempted by evil, and he himself tempts no one' (James 1:13).

Temptation in itself is not sin. Be comforted and encouraged by the fact that the devil finds you worth tempting. Adam and Eve's disobedience brought death to themselves and death to us because of our human nature. Death for Christians, however is birth into God's everlasting kingdom.

We are not alone. As Christians God has given us his Holy Spirit to help and guide us. Christ sympathises with us in our temptations, because he 'was tempted in every way that we are, but did not sin. Let us be brave, then, and approach God's throne, where there is grace. There we will receive mercy and find grace to help us just when we need it' (Hebrews 4:15,16). Christ '... became like man, and appeared in human likeness' (Philippians 2:7). Jesus is helping us every step of the way because he has trodden our path before us and understands our every doubt and every feeling.

Imagine you have fallen off the end of a pier on a wintry day when the sea is rough and icy. You cannot swim, and with the roughness of the sea and intense cold you will not last long. As you are going down for the second time someone drops in alongside you and says, 'I can't swim either but I thought I would keep you company.' You might, if you felt in a state to understand, feel impressed, but you would also feel that it was an extremely foolish act. What you want is a lifesaver, someone who can dive in, and drag you to shore. That person is Jesus who drops in alongside us; the waves are as strong for him as they are for us, the water is as icy for him as it is for us, but he is God-Man. He is not 'identical' to us but can 'identify' with us every step of the way, and because he is also God, he can 'save' us even against the odds.

'Be alert, be on the watch! Your enemy, the Devil, roams round like a roaring lion, looking for someone to devour. Be firm in your faith and resist him, because you know that your fellow-believers in all the world are going through the same kind of sufferings' (1 Peter 5:8,9).

10
In an emergency

ONE
So you're being TEMPTED
TWO
Congratulations!
At least you're *worth* tempting and you *know* you're being tempted.
THREE
Don't let your *feelings* fool you.
Don't be afraid of them – simply don't follow them.
FOUR
Run from the immediacy of the temptation.
In other words move your senses (eyes, ears, taste, etc.) from the centre of the temptation.
FIVE
Pray to God. Distract yourself from the temptation by thanking God for who he is, and for setting you free from guilt and sin.
SIX
Remember the Bible and recall verses that remind you that God is all-powerful in your life. Remember 1 Corinthians 10:13.
SEVEN
Don't get niggled. Just tell the devil to 'Get lost!'

Appendix

Body movement

There are a number of interesting aspects of brain function which deserve our attention in terms of how they work and what affects them.

'Arousal' is a function of the whole brain, but especially of a core of cells which runs up the brain stem into the base of the brain (the 'reticular activating system'). It turns the whole brain 'on' if we are alerted or alarmed, and turns it 'off' during drowsiness and sleep.

'Inhibition' is the mechanism which stops unwise or useless ideas coming through consciousness and out into behaviour. We may feel like hitting someone, but taking stock of the consequences reduces the output to a hostile glance. People mistake inhibition for stimulation, which is why alcoholic drinks used to be called 'stimulants'. In fact alcohol blockades the inhibitory centres in the brain and thus releases the behaviour they were holding back.

'Tension' is a function of parts of the lower brain and certain peripheral nerves (the 'autonomic system'). This has broadly two parts; the 'sympathetic' nervous system transmits aggression and fear, the responses to stress. It is easiest to remember its effects by 'fright, flight and fight', e.g. blood flow increases in muscle but falls in skin and gut, causing drying mouth and failing appetite, a cold sweat, enlarged pupils, and quickened pulse. These are all things which might help someone who needs to fight, or to run from a lion! The other part is the 'parasympathetic' system, which does the opposite; we notice it most easily during a meal, with increased saliva flow and appetite, and a relaxed atmosphere.

Life-style and feelings. Because body and mind are so closely linked, it is no surprise that factors which influence one part affect others; understanding this helps to avoid silly mistakes. For example, shortage of food lowers blood sugar. This in time turns 'on' the sympathetic nervous system. So does coffee. So if I go hungry and have a coffee, I may well end up more tetchy, restless and agitated than I would have been had I eaten. We all know that food relaxes us and we often sleep after a meal. It may be wise to discuss difficult problems over a meal; there is less risk of aggression! Tobacco (or rather the nicotine in it) is more complex; it stimulates and blocks both the sympathetic and parasympathetic nerves. So people find it relieves tension and aids concentration. (Unfortunately it is also quite a strong drug of dependence and a cause of lung cancer, heart disease and bronchitis.)

Tiredness is difficult to evaluate. Its signs are often ignored, someone fails to sleep, tiredness then passes off and they become 'overtired' – a spurious excitement which makes sleep difficult later on, and leaves them feeling very tired the next day. Coffee can also avert tiredness by its stimulant effects. The result is a very nervy, half-awake, uninhibited person who finds it hard to think or to work. Unfortunately it is often others, rather than the sufferer, who recognise the problem. The effects of overtiredness on the body can be considerable; in extreme examples (eg. soldiers, mission doctors) where fighting or work stress extend without sleep over several days, severe illness or even death has occurred. Overtiredness increases 'sympathetic' activity, showing up as 'strain'.

Alcohol is a deceiver (Proverbs 20:1). Some people mistake it for a 'stimulant' when in fact it releases the flood of inappropriate behaviour we call 'drunkenness'. Alcohol is unusual amongst drugs because it is removed from the body by the liver at a fixed rate; this rate varies greatly from person to person, and it is lower in women than in men. Though drinking alcohol is not condemned in the Bible, drunkenness most certainly is, for such behaviour is entirely inconsistent with the life of faith and self-control (Ephesians 5:18). The loss of inhibition is dangerous, partly as a source of provocation to others which easily evokes aggression, partly as a cause of lost sexual control and as a sheer waste of time and resources. Few seem to realise that someone need not be drunk to experience loss of self-control from alcohol. Many a needless argument or unwanted pregnancy has followed. A wise person therefore finds out their own safe level of drinking – not a level recommended by someone else! They avoid excess and never tempt others into it for fun. They will help others out of trouble if they see them losing control. This is 'temperance' (1 Corinthians 9:25) though for some abstinence is the only safe course, and should be respected and not mocked by others.

Sex, like hunger, is an instinctive urge which varies widely from time to time. When Christians speak of love, they mean a caring relationship, a broadly rounded personal commitment, a selfless giving to another. This is *very* different from the world's 'love', which often means a tiny part, and a selfish one, of all that true love can be. It is to do with physical desire, and its satisfaction. It is reduced often to a point where it ceases to be personal, let alone human, and becomes centred on objects. This depersonalised desire is evil, sub-Christian, even sub-human. But it is not hard to see how it happens. There is in all of us (and God alone knows how it comes to be there), an 'image' of attraction, an ideal of the perfect partner. We search out someone near to that image, or just recognise it in someone. But of course that image can never be fulfilled entirely. (Someone's ideal might be fair hair, blue eyes and tall, but the lady he meets may have fair hair, grey eyes and short legs!) This is why it is so important to choose slowly, meet many possible partners, and practise self-control, for once the choice is made it must be one with which we are well content, and one which reflects two people's understanding of one another's personalities. Sadly, instead of this many people choose on impulse, discovering later that what moved their choice was some fragment, a laugh, a bathing costume, a kind deed – something which in no way disclosed a whole personality. This is rather like giving someone a transfusion of blood with only one group matched – and like it, it is a sure road to trouble! Sex desire is increased by anything which congests the pelvis (and this can be anything from constipation or a full bladder to tight clothing). It is also 'turned on' by suggestive or revealing dress, reading material or films and close physical contact with other people. The problem is that arousal, once triggered, tends to 'lock on' and increase, demanding satisfaction. We have seen how hunger increases 'sympathetic' desire; if the surroundings dictate fear or stress, sex drive departs. However, if the circumstances are relaxed it tends rather to increase, such is the complexity of the sex controls.

All this amounts to the fact that a caring Christian, who wants a controlled but full and happy life lived in God's way, will take pains to identify and avoid situations which tend to 'turn on' desire in themselves, or in others, when that desire cannot be fulfilled in the loving way God created. This way involves gradual growth into a caring relationship. In many cultures this will follow the course of friendship, courtship, engagement and marriage – all the steps of growing commitment. In other cultures the order may differ but the principle remains. This is the only responsible relationship into which children may eventually be born, the family.

This clearly raises difficulties for young, single Christians who are most likely to find themselves in problem situations. It is so important for them not to confuse the world's 'love' with the real thing. The world's 'love' may be no more than a confused impulse which owes more to how someone may have eaten, drunk or worked than to anything else. This is why some people seem always to be falling in (and out of) 'love', and leaving a trail of scarred people behind them.

The person of the world is controlled by feelings; what he wants *now* seems to determine right and wrong, and certainly governs what he will do (Ephesians 2:1–3). Christians take a different view, knowing that desires are often transient and may depend on little more than blood chemistry. They will want to have 'the mind of Christ', a mind which is submitted to God's will and to reasoned principles.